GO WITH THE FLOW

Go With the Flow:

A non-religious approach to your daily time with God

Copyright © 2014, Brightheart Resources

All quotations from the Bible are taken from *The Holy Bible: New International Version* ®. NIV®. Copyright © 1984, by International Bible Society.

Endorsements

"Brad makes spending time with Jesus accessible and user-friendly, and even more than that, he actually makes it make sense. Using the template of Tabernacle worship, Brad breaks down the different aspects of being with God in a way that is appealing whether you've been a Christ follower 1 year or 31 years. He talks about "approaching God in God's way" and as a person raised in the church, I've never heard about time spent with God talked about in such a unique way. Go with the Flow is a smart, easy-to-read book that will help you meet Jesus in a new way."

~ Sarah Markley, freelance writer and speaker (Go check out her beautifully written—and hugely popular—blog at sarahmarkley.com.)

"In this precious little book Brad Huebert reveals a radical approach to approaching God. A simple…yet profound…concept that provides for a much deeper, more genuine prayer life. This may very well change your quiet time forever."

~ Michael K. Reynolds, author of the acclaimed Heirs of Ireland Series (Check out Michael's website and other books at michaelkreynolds.com.)

Acknowledgements

This may be a little book, but it can make a huge impact. So thank you, Lord Jesus—for paving the way and paying my way to have eternal life with you—a life that starts now in you and will never end because you never end. I love you so much!

I also want to thank some people for their part in helping me get this project off the ground.

First of all, thanks to James MacDonald and his thought-provoking book, *Vertical Church*. God used you to reawaken me to the fact that the Bible does, in fact, champion a flow of worship that glorifies God and is really good for us.

Thank you Shauna, for believing in me and marrying me and loving me through all the ups and downs of my writing journey. Back at ya!

Thanks also go to Marla Pearce and Lindsay Franklin for their generous offer to proofread my work on this project.

Thank you Michael K. Reynolds and Sarah Markley, for writing such kind and thoughtful endorsements.

Thank you, Kim Bangs, for writing such a personal foreword for the book.

And thank you, reader, for buying this book.

Foreword

I've been walking this journey with Jesus for over 35 years. Yes, I did start out as a very young gal.

Somehow (and I wasn't taught this), I ended up as a do's and don'ts Christian. Everything for me was about rules and following them to the nth degree. If I failed, I had to go back to start, put on another ankle weight, and try again.

My quiet time was supposed to be precious—a daily time with Him, spending time in the Word, in worship and prayer, building a relationship with Him.

I've done the SOAP method, the PRAY method, the must read the Bible through in a year method, and any and every other method I heard about. I'm not saying these methods in themselves are not a great way to learn and focus. However, when the method becomes the worshipped, then we've got a problem.

Imagine (or maybe you've experienced) you wake, do what you must, and then go to your quiet time location. You follow your method or plan, only to doze off, not have time to complete the plan, lose focus—whatever it may be. So the result: you leave your quiet place more weighted down than when you arrived. And that, my friend, is not God's plan.

Having lost my ability to "enjoy" my daily time with the Lord and having become so guilt-laden for not reading enough, praying long enough, missing a day, not journaling—desperation arose. It was either quit altogether or discover a new way of doing things.

Enjoy became a key word...recognizing that the "quiet time" was a greater desire of the Father's than of mine! You cannot have a solid relationship with anyone if you don't spend time with them, talking to them, learning about them and *listening* to them.

My radical thought was if God sent His Son Jesus to pay the price for my sins in order to restore relationship with me, than perhaps my time with the Lord should be about that relationship instead of time spent so I could check something off my to-do list.

Since I made that change, what a joy my time with God has become. Yes, I have that time daily at a time of day that works best for me and my life. At home, on the road, on vacation, on a business trip, in a hotel room, in someone else's home. Every day, everywhere…why? Because I so look forward to the moments I spend with Him. It is the absolute delight of my day. Not every day is the same; not every day do I feel like I'm walking on the mountain top. But, every day, I do *know* that I've been with my God. My King. The one who loves me no matter what and always will.

News flash: it just isn't for me or for Brad who wrote this book. Each one of us who has begun a personal relationship with Jesus can have that kind of daily time with Him and the Father.

In the pages of *Go With The Flow*, you'll discover that God-ordained pattern of our time spent with Him. He laid it out many years ago with the children of Israel and it serves as a model for us today.

The truths in this book will be revolutionary to most (if not all). As I read the book, my passion for my time with God was rekindled. I've gained some new focus. I'm looking forward to adding what I've learned to my time.

Brad makes a bold declaration in the Introduction: "This little book is going to help you grow the daily devotional time with God you've longed for all your life. Seriously."

Shake off the old mindsets (and if you don't have any, you're already a step ahead). Read these pages…slowly, absorb. Read the text of the Bible as well. Dig deep…the water in the re-dug well is fresh, refreshing, and life changing.

Go with the flow!

Kim Bangs
Publishing Director, Gospel Light / Regal Books

Introduction

First things first.

If you've been a Christ-follower for a while and want to figure out how to get more out of your daily quiet time with God, **read this introduction first.**

If you've recently become a Christ-follower and have no idea what a daily quiet time is, skip this section and **start with chapter one.** That way you can jump ahead of all the long-time super-Christians you know. You're welcome.

****

Imagine sitting with me over coffee at a local Starbucks. After a typical "So, how's life?" conversation, I lean in real close and ask, "How is your quiet time with God going lately?"

You hesitate. Embarrassment—no, more like shame—creeps up the back of your neck. You look down, fiddle with your stir stick. Brush a few crumbs from the table top.

At this point you're going to describe one of two problems: Disconnect, or a rut. Here's what I mean by disconnect.

"My walk with God?" you reply. "It's okay, I guess. But not great."

"No? What do you mean by that?"

You look up. "I mean, I don't exactly do my devotions regularly. Or much at all."

"Why not?"

You size me up. Decide to trust me. "To be honest, I don't really get much out of them." The shame intensifies, like a wet blanket draped over your shoulders. "I don't feel very close to God."

"Sorry to hear that."

"Every once and a while I try to reboot some kind of daily routine with God but it never lasts. To be honest, I don't have a clue what I'm supposed to be doing. So I just kinda settle for less. Which isn't much."

Or maybe you'd describe a spiritual rut.

"My walk with God? I do my daily devotions most the time, if that's what you mean."

"Well, good for you. But that's not what I'm poking at."

"It isn't?"

"No. I mean, how are you and God *doing?* As in, your relationship."

"Like I said, I do my devotions every day."

"Okay, but do you enjoy them? Do you experience God while you're spending time with him? Are you growing? Does it give you joy?"

"Well, I'm in the middle of a dry season, I guess. But I'm doing my best."

"How long has this dry season been going on?"

You sigh. "A really long time. But I don't know what else to do, or how to fix it."

Regardless of which track you identify with most, I've got very good news. This little book is going to help you grow the daily devotional time with God you've longed for all your life. Seriously. Imagine:

- Exchanging your dutiful "ought to" motive for a passionate "need to."
- Leaving behind the lukewarm land of "want to" to explore the promised land of "love to."
- Being washed by the grace and love of God every day.
- Pouring out your soul to God and being filled with his holy presence.
- Gaining God's daily perspective on your relationships, your career, and your calling.
- A Bible that comes alive in your hands and shapes your life.
- Actually becoming more like Jesus Christ over time.

- Daily time with God that leaves you refreshed and focused, full of faith and peace.
- Expecting to meet with God every single day and not being disappointed.

More good news: God wants this for you more than you want it for yourself. And you won't need a seminary degree to make this work. You don't even have to particularly intelligent, spiritual, or even self-disciplined.

What you *will* need:

- You'll have to be fully and delightfully...human. And honest about that. Us being human and God being God is the heart of our time with him. Notice I said human, not religious.

- Willingness to *un*-learn some things. Lots of things, actually. And relearn God's truth along the way. Because lots of what you've been fed about your walk with God is not only wrong, it's been killing your devotional life and dooming it to failure.

- You'll need to put aside any devotional books you're currently reading and get your Bible ready. Yeah, I know. But it'll be great. Let's get started.

Chapter 1
Go with the flow

I set aside quiet time to spend with God every single day. See, Jesus isn't just our ticket to heaven or even just our lifeline here and now. He is our *life itself* (Colossians 3:3,4). Without God, we're spiritually dead in the water. The more we live saturated with him and his love, the more alive we are.

If we want the full life Jesus came to give us (John 10:10), we have to live in him and he in us, like a branch growing on a grapevine (John 15:1-8). Which means every single day, we need to spend some time entirely focused on him and the life he's trying to give us. I call this space set aside just for God my *quiet time.*

During my own quiet time, I regularly experience the grace and love of God in a tangible way. I hear God's voice and gain his perspective on my life. His written word shapes my mind, my decisions, and the effect my life has on others. I become more like Jesus and learn to embrace my new self in Christ. I let go of burdens and find freedom from fear and sin. I pray with faith and surrender myself again to God's plan for me. When I'm done I find myself refreshed, focused, and full of faith and peace.

Every single day, I expect to meet in a special way with the God of the universe, and I'm never disappointed. And here's the thing: I don't have a quiet time because I ought to. I do it because I need to. I don't just *want* to spend time with Jesus; I *love* spending time with Jesus. Which is how it should be. And you need to know, I'm not sugar coating my experience. This is what my quiet time consistently looks and feels like. It's what your quiet time can look and feel like, too.

In case you're wondering, my experience with God isn't super-spiritual. I don't have any special in with God that you can't have through simple faith. What I'm enjoying with God is supposed to be normal. So here's my promise: If you follow the instructions I'm going to share over the next few chapters, your quiet time with God will become the best and most important part of every day you live. It will supercharge your life with God's power and purpose.

The key, as you've probably guessed, lies in spending your quiet time doing what God wants you to do, how he wants you to do it. And he's laid that out clearly in the Bible. I'll show you what I mean.

In Genesis chapter 12 in the Old Testament God calls a guy named Abraham to be his right hand man, the first recruit for what would eventually become his chosen nation—Israel. After waiting a few hundred years for Abraham's offspring to multiply into a sizeable group of people, God approached them with a calling and a special kind of blueprint.

In the book of Exodus from chapter 25 through 31, God showed Israel (the ancient Hebrews) how to build a tabernacle (a portable temple) where he promised he would meet with them and be their God.

Later in their history, once they had established themselves in their own land, he told them to build a permanent and impressive stonework Temple there. It was laid out with the same basic blueprint as the tabernacle and accomplished the very same purpose: A place to meet with God.

But here's the really cool part: The Tabernacle/Temple not only created a *place* to meet with God, but a *pathway* or flow to follow while meeting with him. The pathway was unmistakable because it was built into the structure of the Temple itself. Here's a rough diagram that illustrates how the Temple (and the flow of worship) was laid out:

Based on this clear.God-given blueprint, the Hebrew flow of worship had five parts. You can see them clearly laid out in the diagram on the next page:

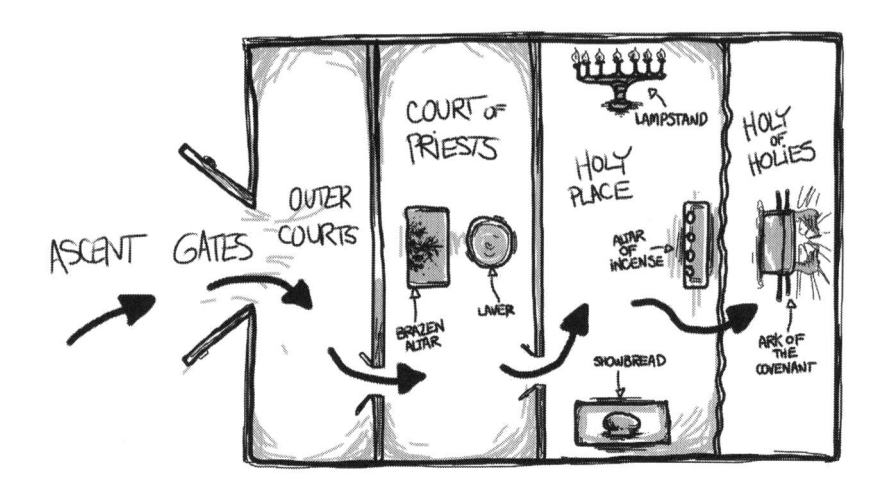

Ascent

The Temple was located in Jerusalem, a walled city perched on a massive hill. Pilgrims would converge on Jerusalem from all over the Judean countryside to worship at the Temple, which involved ascending the hill to get there.

Pilgrims took advantage of their trek up the hill to reflect on what was on their minds and give it over to God in prayer. They used a "songbook" found in Psalms 120-134 to help them focus their ascent.

Entering through the gates into the courtyards

When the worshippers reached the city and passed through the gates into the outer courtyards of the Temple, they thanked and praised God for who he is and what he had done for them.

The altar and sacrifices

Only the priests and Levites could enter this court. It's where animals were sacrificed to God to atone for the sins of the people. A giant laver (a bronze basin of water) also stood ready, where the priests washed their hands of the blood and gore.

The Holy Place

The Holy Place housed three pieces of furniture: A table with a fresh loaf of bread on it, symbolizing the promise of God's care and provision; a golden, seven-pronged lamp stand, perpetually lit, that symbolized the promise of God's eternal presence with them; and an altar where incense was offered to God along with the prayers of the priests on behalf of the people.

The Holy of Holies

The Holy of Holies was curtained off because the Ark of the Covenant was kept there. God himself would appear between two gold sculpted angelic beings (cherubim) who flanked the cover of the ark. Only the High Priest could enter the Holy of Holies, just once per year, and only after all the proper sacrifices and preparations. Even then, they often tied a rope around the guy's ankle just in case he didn't get it all right and God struck him dead. That way they could drag his body back out without sending anyone else in to die. Seriously, it was pretty crazy.

So....

What does this have to do with us today? Well, I used to claim, "Nothing in the Bible tells us how to spend our quiet time with God." But I was wrong. The Temple does exactly that. A good chunk of the Old Testament revolves around this flow of worship and how people used it to approach God in God's way.

At this point someone is going to point out that everything I've explained so far is found in the *Old Testament*. And that's true. You might also remind me that Jesus fulfilled the whole Temple system as the promised Messiah. And you'd be right. But in the book of Hebrews, the writer spends several chapters explaining what Christ accomplished and how that impacts how we approach God.

After explaining the Temple structure and flow we've just been talking about in Hebrews 9:1-10, he says,

> "When Christ came as the high priest of the things that are already here, he went through the greater and more perfect tabernacle that is not man-made, that is to say, not a part of this creation. He did not enter by the means of the blood of goats and calves, but entered the Most Holy Place once for all by his own blood, having obtained eternal redemption" (Hebrews 9:11,12).

In other words, the earthly tabernacle and Temple were patterned after a spiritual or heavenly tabernacle. Hebrews 10:1 says "The law is only a shadow of the good things that are coming — not the realities themselves."

The second thing to notice is that Jesus, the author and perfecter of our faith himself used the "Temple flow" of the heavenly reality to fulfill his promises to us (Hebrews 12:2). It's that important. But did Jesus' fulfillment of the flow make it obsolete? No, exactly the opposite; he injected it with life and power:

> "Therefore, brothers, since we have confidence to enter the most Holy Place by the blood of Jesus, by a new and living way opened for us through the curtain, that is, his body, and since we have a great high priest over the house of God, let us draw near to God with a sincere heart in full assurance of faith, having our hearts sprinkled to cleanse us from a guilty conscience and having our bodies washed with pure water. Let us hold unswervingly to the hope we profess, for he who promised is faithful" (Hebrews 10:18-22).

Did you catch that? We're supposed to approach God, to "draw near" to him, through this new and living *way* opened up for us through Jesus. So there is a specific *way* ordained by God. And while it's based on the Old Testament Temple, Christ's way is still very much alive.

If all we had to go on was a construction blueprint for an Old Testament order of service, we should probably just ignore it. But what we have, friends, is a flow of worship fulfilled and empowered by Jesus Christ himself. Because of his work on the cross, this approach is now laced with life and grace; it's become everything it was designed to be, and *it still stands for you today.*

In Christ, the Old Testament Temple flow is fulfilled but not forgotten. The old songbook becomes a new springboard. The sacrifices offered *by* us are replaced by Jesus and his once-for-all sacrifice *for* us. The physical place becomes a spiritual posture. What were originally hoops to jump through in order to satisfy God become helps that satisfy the deepest needs of our souls. The symbols take on substance. The Ark of the Covenant is replaced by the throne of grace (Hebrews 4:16).

Incredible, don't you think?

It's true that God is everywhere—that in Christ, we have access to the Father no matter where we are, at any time. There's nothing stopping you from praying in the car on the way to work, or reading your Bible during a five minute break before getting back to work after lunch. The Holy Spirit can and does speak to us during the busiest times of our lives. He touches and helps us while we're knee deep in the mucky trenches of real life, in real time. Praise God.

But access doesn't equal intimacy. Just because we can connect with God doesn't mean we do. Even if we do connect with God it doesn't mean we're connecting in a meaningful way. You know this. It's probably one of the reasons you're reading this book.

You might also be thinking, "You said this was going to be a non-religious approach to having a quiet time. Isn't basing the whole thing on the Old Testament as religious as it gets?" Well, as I've just shown, this isn't an Old Testament thing. It's an eternal, kingdom of God thing. But let me take it a step further: When Jesus Christ launched his public ministry, John the Baptist, a prophet sent to prepare the way for him, was thrown in jail.

Understandably, John was left wondering, "Is this guy the real deal? I need to know, because I'm probably going to die in here." When Jesus heard about John's doubts, he replied, "Go back to John and report what you hear and see: The blind receive sight, the lame walk, those who have leprosy are cleansed, the deaf hear, the dead are raised, and the good news is proclaimed to the poor" (Matthew 11:4,5). In other words, "Look at the fruit."

Before you launch into this approach to your time with God, you may need to know whether this is the real deal too. So let me share with you what I see and hear about going with the flow. In my own life, God is consistently using it to:

- Help me get over myself every day
- Cleanse my conscience of guilt and shame
- Focus my eyes on Jesus and what matters to him
- Help me live my entire life with God's perspective, in his presence, with his power
- Release my heart from yesterday's burdens
- Tune me in to his voice and guidance
- Free my mind of tomorrow's worries
- Help me enjoy God and develop a grateful, worshipful heart
- Give me a space, even for just a few minutes a day, where I can simply adore, behold, and enjoy God for who he is instead of what he can do for me
- Send me into my day as his hands and feet

If you want to experience God's love and power every day, you can. He's left the front door open and handed you the Temple flow to walk you through it. Scripture says the *way* Jesus fulfilled helps us approach God with a sincere heart in full assurance of faith. That's why I promise that if you approach God in God's way during your quiet time, you'll experience an intimacy with God you've only dreamed of until now.

Think of it: God introduced this way to approach him in the tabernacle. He then underlined it in the Temple. Eventually Jesus illustrated this way yet again through his death and resurrection. And finally, God reminds us in the book of Hebrews that Christ's living way still stands, ready for us to embrace personally. In other words, the Temple flow helps us live out and apply the gospel of Jesus Christ.

The obvious question is, why aren't we using Jesus' way to connect with God every single day? I think it's because we didn't know we could. Now we do! But I also think it's because we don't know how to walk that path. So here's the deal: If you stay with me, each chapter of this book will help you get over one more "how-to" hump once and for all.

Like a fish in a river, it's time to go with the flow.

Chapter 2
Ascent

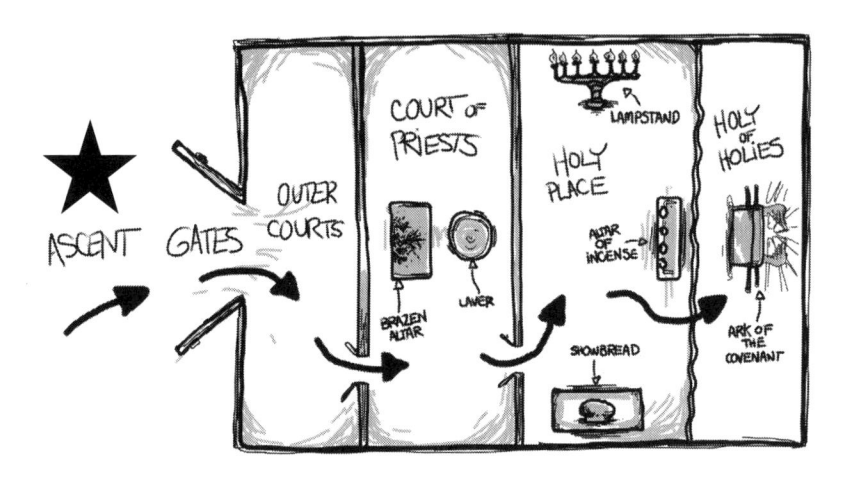

The first thing you need to know about spending time with God is this:

You get to be human.

When you spend time with God, you get to be yourself. You get to feel what you feel, wrestle with your issues, vent like a madperson and be completely honest about the shameful crud you can't seem to get off your mind. You can cry, laugh, blow off steam, and completely lose it. In other words, you get to come as you are, wherever your heart happens to be.

No, wait—it's not that you *get to be human*. You actually *need to* be human if your quiet time is going to become the rich source of life you want it to be.

Unfortunately, that's not how most people approach their time with God. For most of my life I'd sit down with my Bible and put on my best spiritual attitude and try to connect with God from there. In other words, I tried to elevate myself into God's presence by thinking godly thoughts. Quiet time was "holy time."

Truthfully, I think I picked up the habit in church. How many Sunday mornings have you heard a well-meaning pastor or worship leader say, "Okay, welcome here this morning. Let's just lay aside all our struggles now, all our conflict, all our issues. Let's put them down for an hour and focus our eyes on Jesus." And how many times have you tried to do that? Tried to leave your junk at the door so you could really dial down and meet with God?

It sounds so spiritual, so right. Jesus is worthy, he's awesome, so get over yourself. It's holy time, people.

That's not spiritual, it's just religious. While religion strives to ascend toward God, the message of the gospel is that God condescends to us. Jesus "became flesh and dwelt among us" (John 1:14). Paul says Jesus "made himself nothing by taking the very nature of a servant, being made in human likeness. And being found in appearance as a man, he humbled himself by becoming obedient to death—even death on a cross!" (Philippians 2:7,8). God meets you where you're at so he can lift you up to where he is. That's what the gospel does.

Your quiet time doesn't require you being on your best behaviour. That's religion, not the gospel! Shutting your needs out of your prayer and worship sends the message that your faith has precious little to do with your actual life. But God wants you to be absolutely real so he can meet you in the trenches where life happens.

This is critical: Jesus doesn't want you to leave your junk at the door before coming in. He wants you to drag the whole stinking mess with you into his presence so he can saturate it with his awesomeness. The "holy time" attitude is deadly because it misses the whole point of having a quiet time—learning to live your whole life in God. It also robs you of the most natural place to start: again, your actual life.

Jesus says, "I am the Vine, and you are the branches. If you abide in me and I abide in you, you will bear much fruit" (John 15:5). To abide means to *live in*, not just to think focused, spiritual thoughts about. "If you live your entire life in me," Jesus is saying,

"I will live the fullness of my life through you and together we'll change the world." Wow.

I think the "holy time" mentality is also why people tend to buy devotional books instead of studying the Bible for themselves. We're basically hiring people more spiritually-minded than we are to give us more profound spiritual thoughts to think, more spiritual prayers to pray, and a clever spiritual thought we could never come up with ourselves to guide our day. I read Christian books all the time, but they can't replace one on one time with my Lord and Saviour.

If you've worked through a devotional book you've probably experienced moments when you read the daily ditty and thought, "Wow, that's crazy. This is just what I needed today!" Amazing, right? It's humbling that the God of the universe would orchestrate things so that a specific devotional entry would hit you where you live right when you need it. That's how he rolls. But listen: Getting hit between the eyes is going to be rare if you're trying to connect with God using material downloaded from someone else's head space while living a completely different life than you're living. Right?

Hear me on this: Your quiet time is supposed to hit you where you live *every single time.* A quiet time that speaks directly to your current experience should never surprise you. If you want God to hit you where you live, then where you live is where to begin.

Ascent

So let's talk about the launch pad for your quiet time: *ascent.*

Like I mentioned earlier, as Hebrew pilgrims ascended the hill toward Jerusalem they reflected on what was on their minds and gave it over to God in prayer. They often used Psalms 120 through 134 like an ancient version of Pinterest: an "idea book" to get them started.

- Psalms 124 and 126 focus on relishing a **God-moment** or **answer to prayer.**
- Psalm 128 unpacks **a truth** God has been teaching the writer.

- Psalm 129 celebrates **a victory** over a recent struggle.
- Psalm 120 walks through **a current problem** weighing on the writer's heart.
- Psalms 121, 125, and 127 start with **a metaphor** for our walk with God and unpack the implications.
- Psalm 123 and 131 unpack **relational images** (master/slave, mother/child) in prayer.
- Psalm 130 unravels **a fresh sin** the writer committed, including how they feel about it.

If you don't know where to start in your quiet time, try a few of these biblical springboards and you'll be swimming in the deep end in no time.

Personally, I rarely use the Psalms of ascent—not because they aren't great places to start, but because my life is already on my mind and that's what ascent is all about. Which means their "ascent springboard" list isn't exhaustive. For example, try starting your quiet time with these gems:

Complaints. I'm serious. If you don't grumble *to* God, you'll just end up grumbling *against* God. One is welcomed as part of the conversation (Psalm 142:1,2; John 6:61). The other is sin (Numbers 14:27).

Frustration and anger. Like when life's not working out. Or people are being stupid and hurtful. Or even when you're mad at God (Jeremiah 4:10).

Physical pain, sickness, or other struggles. Like your chronic migraines. The flu going around. Your aching back. Your lousy sleep last night.

Fears, worries, and anxiety (Philippians 4:6,7). The critical meeting you're obsessing about. What the lump on your shoulder is made of. Whether the new couple will like you.

Questions, confusion, and doubts. Remember how patient the resurrected Jesus was with "doubting" Thomas? "Here, stick your finger in where the spear gored me. Nasty, huh? But I'm better now" (John 20:27).

Temptations. Like the co-worker you feel drawn to. The internet site you shouldn't visit again. The last piece of cake in the fridge. Jesus modelled praying about temptation in the garden of Gethsemane.

The great thing is, nothing is off limits. Remember, you're trying to live your entire life saturated by God, so you need to bring your entire life to God so he can saturate it. To help you see what I mean, here's what I wrote to God during my "ascent" a few days ago. Word for word:

- Okay, my back SUCKS. Truly. It's pretty discouraging and limiting. Help!
- I'm thankful for a slow day in a slower rest of the week.
- I want to write some more today. And get to the heart of it.
- I want to clean house today (or at least part of it) to bless Shauna.

That's it. My ascent stuff for October 23rd. No angels singing (that I could hear, anyway), no epic theme music swelling to accommodate the awesomeness of my disclosure. Just me being real.

A friend of mine recently tried this temple flow idea for her quiet time. She told me during her ascent zone her brain kept channel surfing: "And this, and this, and that, and this, and the other thing..." She was concerned that she'd never get to the end of the venting session because so many things kept popping into her mind. Maybe you can relate to her experience.

Don't worry; you're not infinite, so you'll exhaust yourself eventually.

The real reason you have a hundred and forty-two things on your list is you've let them accumulate in your soul. They're like a giant pile of leaves growing in your brain. Every time you open the door to God, the wind of his Spirit swirls them up into a crazy mess. If you raked up every stray thought and bagged them with

God every day, there wouldn't be so many to deal with at one time. You'd probably have five or six or maybe ten.

And the bottom line is, those things matter to God anyway. This paradigm shift is profound: Those stupid things that keep popping into your mind aren't distractions; they're the point. They're your path towards intimacy with God.

"Uh, but most of the things on my mind aren't very spiritual." No, they're probably not. But they're real, so sharing them with God is being real about what's on your mind. Remember, too, that our ascent is just the launch pad. We won't stay there for long. God meets us where we are so he can take us where he is. We learn to go "higher up and further in," to borrow a phrase from the Chronicles of Narnia.

Don't get me wrong; your life isn't all about you, it's about Jesus. One of the most pressing needs you have is to get over yourself. And you will, if you go with the flow. It's just that the only way to get over yourself is to give yourself to him. All of yourself. Starting with what's already eating you alive is also practical. It's on your mind anyway! God knows that, and he'd rather help you get it off your chest than pretend it isn't there and fight against it the whole time you're together.

More importantly, unspooling your tangled reality is the first (and non-negotiable) step towards giving everything to God and living your entire existence saturated with who he is. If you don't start by being real, how can you expect a real experience with him?

Admit it, I have a point.

One last note: Did you notice how brief my own venting notes were? "I want to write some more today. And get to the heart of it. I want to clean house today (or at least part of it) to bless Shauna." The principle is this: Be specific enough with your venting that you feel a weight off your chest for sharing, and brief enough that you don't get stuck in the mud.

This is important. During your ascent you're being real, which is fantastic—but you're not exactly thinking or believing straight at this point. Processing your issues in your current headspace would probably just feed your flesh. The focus of the ascent phase is moving your thoughts and feelings from introspection to prayer, but not prayer *requests* quite yet.

Here's why: A prayer request is telling God how you think he should resolve the issues you're facing. Many times, you've already got some pretty clear ideas about that: "Dear Lord, please cause my idiot boss to get hit by a blimp." Which may or may not be God's best for you. Or for your boss.

Starting with the issue and parking there before asking for stuff gives God the space to peel back the layers, to expose what's really going on: *Perhaps wanting your boss to die a horrible death won't solve your problem; perhaps that sentiment says something important about your heart.* And don't worry—you'll come back to all the stuff you've logged later on, in the *Holy Place*, when you're tracking with God and his purposes for you.

Recently another friend of mine tried to put this Temple flow concept into action during his quiet time. I say *tried* because he started twice but never got farther than the ascent zone. Life happens, right? He resolved to go deeper the following week, but then added that it still felt amazing to pour out all the stuff splashing around in his brain in the presence of God. Even though he never got further than that, he was still pleased with his experience with God that week. As he should have been.

Like him, though, you're ready for the next step.

Chapter 3
Thank You, Praise You

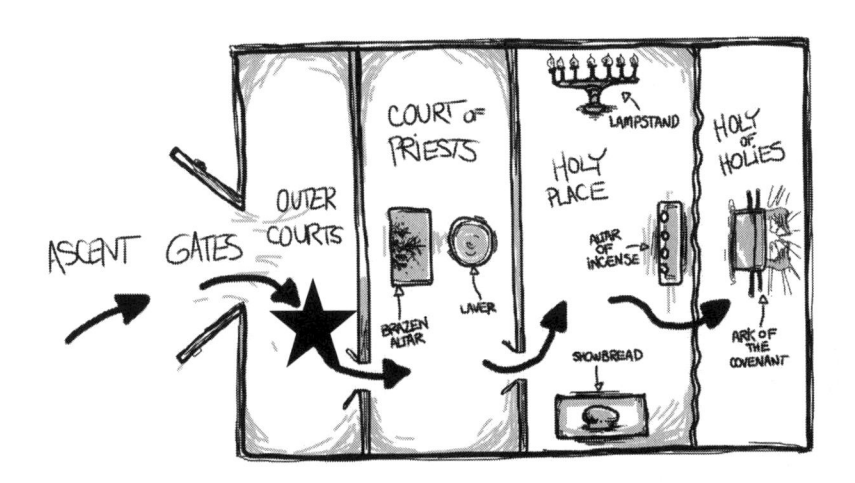

The paradox of the last chapter is this: You think your life is about you, but it's not. God knows that, and lets you start there, with yourself…but he wants you to get past yourself.

Hebrew worshippers ascending toward Jerusalem experienced what you'll also find, if you give raw ascent a try: a change in perspective. As we convert our introspective blather into prayer, a massive shift occurs in little steps: Our soul blinks, comes out of its stupor, stops looking at itself, and starts looking up to God. In this famous ascent song, the Psalm writer says, "I lift my eyes up to the hills—where does my help come from? My help comes from the Lord, the Maker of heaven and earth" (Psalm 121:1,2).

Mission accomplished.

The best way to get over yourself is to focus on something outside yourself. In particular, to cultivate a thankful, praise-filled heart toward God. By the time the venting Hebrews arrived at the Temple gates, their minds had begun to comprehend the larger story unfolding in their lives and God's supreme place in it. Check this out:

> Shout for joy to the Lord, all the earth. Worship the Lord with gladness; come before him with joyful songs. Know that the Lord is God. It is he who made us, and we are his; we are his people, the sheep of his pasture. Enter his gates with thanksgiving and his courts with praise; give thanks to him and praise his name. For the Lord is good and his love endures forever; his faithfulness continues through all generations (Psalm 100).

So vent and complain and talk up your life with God. Do the ascent thing. Absolutely. But at some point, as you reach the Temple gates, pause before you go in. Stop in your tracks and ask God to help you take an inventory of your life. What are you thankful for? What should you praise him for?

Again, don't be religious, be real. Think about the last twenty-four hours, and let the thanks flow.

Thank him for answers to prayer, for special moments with friends and family. Thank him for cinnamon buns and warm jackets in fall. Thank him for encouragement that found its way past your walls, for laughter and life and salvation. Thank him for difficult things too, trusting him to work all things for your good because you love him and are called according to his purpose. Thank him for strength, for what he's teaching you, for how you're changing and growing in your faith. Thank him for his grace, his patience, his awesomeness, that he's even listening to you at all.

Obvious, right? You've heard all this before.

But what do we do when life is hard? What if you're going through a dark valley full of confusion, loneliness, and pain? What if you've just experienced a grievous loss, a crippling wound, a discouraging failure? What if you don't feel particularly thankful?

What if you can't think of much to praise God for? What if you don't want to?

Yeah, that's a tough one. But my advice is both biblical and scientific. Many recent studies have proven that an attitude of gratitude is good for us, even (and especially) when life is painful. So to begin with, try giving thanks for your own good. But let's also open ourselves to a little perspective.

The Apostle Paul had it rough too. Imagine having the following conversation with him. All Paul's responses are pulled directly from II Corinthians 11:23-33:

> You: I've been working really hard. Too hard.
> Paul: **I have worked much harder.**
> I can honestly say, my job feels like a prison most days.
> **I've been in prison—real prison—frequently.**
> It's just that...well, I'm really taking a beating in my life right now.
> **I've been flogged. Severely.**
> I find it really hard. I do. For one thing, I'm continually exposed to my idiot manager's issues in the office.
> **I've been exposed to death again and again.**
> No, but it's been absolutely brutal. My boss gave me a tongue-lashing last week.
> **Five times I received from the Jews the forty lashes minus one.**
> Not only that, my mutual funds have taken a real beating this quarter.
> **Three times I was beaten with rods.**
> And then—not cool—my brand new car got pelted by hail on Thursday while I was away on business. I mean, come on, God.
> **Once I was pelted with stones.**
> If I'd been home on time, I could have parked the car in the garage, but no! On my way home from the business trip on Thursday, my plane was delayed so I missed my connecting flight.
> **Three times, I was shipwrecked.**

Okay, and then... this is rich... I had to spend the night and most of the next day in a cheap hotel without a continental breakfast or a pool. I'm just saying.

I spent a night and a day in the open sea.

I'd say it was the cherry on top of a brutal year where the stupid economy ruined our financial picture and forced us to move into a cheaper home.

I have been constantly on the move.

Seriously, though. I'm in danger of losing my mind. If I have to attend another funeral, I'm going to melt down.

I have been in danger from rivers, in danger from bandits, in danger from my fellow Jews, in danger from Gentiles; in danger in the city, in danger in the country, in danger at sea; and in danger from false believers.

I mean, it's more common than not that I hit the pillow at the end of the day completely exhausted.

I have laboured and toiled and have often gone without sleep.

And another thing! I'm getting sick of bag lunches. If I see another ham sandwich, I'm going to flush it down the toilet. I really will.

I have known hunger and thirst and have often gone without food.

While we're on this track, my spring jacket—the navy blue one with the nice pockets? Yeah. It's got a hole in the sleeve.

I have been cold and naked.

I could go on and on. My family obligations are overwhelming. My kids are always like, "Daddy, daddy!" I never get a break.

Besides everything else, I face daily the pressure of my concern for all the churches.

Tomorrow is Monday. I hate Mondays. My secretary always corners me with all the paperwork I need to catch up on. Blah blah blah... I feel so trapped.

In Damascus... the governor under King Aretas had the city of the Damascenes guarded in order to arrest me.

But last week, it was brilliant. I slipped away from her by scooting under my buddy's desk before she saw me. Not pretty, but effective.

I was lowered in a basket from a window in the wall.

No offense, but I think Paul wins the pity party contest. And this same guy, the poster boy for suffering and "bad days at the office" says this: "Give thanks in all circumstances; for this is God's will for you in Christ Jesus" (I Thessalonians 5:18). All circumstances. Even the hard ones. And those aren't just pretty words. Once, during a ministry trip, a crowd turned on Paul while he was preaching and things went south in a big way:

> The crowd joined in the attack against Paul and Silas, and the magistrates ordered them to be stripped and beaten. After they had been severely flogged, they were thrown into prison, and the jailer was commanded to guard them carefully. Upon receiving such orders, he put them in the inner cell and fastened their feet in the stocks. About midnight Paul and Silas were praying and singing hymns to God, and the other prisoners were listening to them. Suddenly there was such a violent earthquake that the foundations of the prison were shaken. At once all the prison doors flew open, and everybody's chains came loose. (Acts 16:22-26)

Incredible, right? Paul landed in jail for doing what God told him to do. He was beaten and locked up because of his love for Jesus. And what does he do? He prays. He sings. "Thank you, praise you."

Was he insane?

Nope. What happened next?

God shook the foundations of the prison, the doors flew open, and the chains came loose.

You're saying, "Good for him. But I've taken a beating, I'm in a dark place, I'm hurting, and I'm feeling betrayed and forgotten by

God. My life feels like a prison. I don't have anything to praise God for. I'm not thankful, I'm bitter."

I'm not saying you haven't taken a beating. I'm not saying you aren't hurt. I'm not saying life isn't dark, that you aren't in chains, that what happened to you is fair.

I'm saying that turning your bitterness into praise will shake the foundation of the prison you're in.

I'm saying that thanking him for his goodness—even if it means thanking him that your left foot shackle isn't as tight as your right foot shackle—is going to open the prison doors.

I'm saying looking to God with a grateful heart for his love and faithfulness is going to loosen those heavy chains.

I'm saying that giving God thanks dispels darkness, begins the healing process, and clears the path for a new day.

If you're finding that hard, you're not alone. But it's time to sit down and have a chat with your soul. David shows us how it's done:

> Praise the Lord, O my soul; all my inmost being, praise his holy name. Praise the Lord, O my soul, and forget not all his benefits—who forgives all your sins, and heals all your diseases, who redeems your life from the pit and crowns you with love and compassion, who satisfies your desires with good things so that your life is renewed like the eagle's. (Psalm 103:1-5).

Ascend, and vent to Jesus as you go. Then enter his courts with praise and give him thanks for who he is and what he's done. Sit for a while and relish the good stuff with a grateful heart to God.

But we're not done yet. In fact, it's just getting interesting.

Chapter 4
Sacrifice

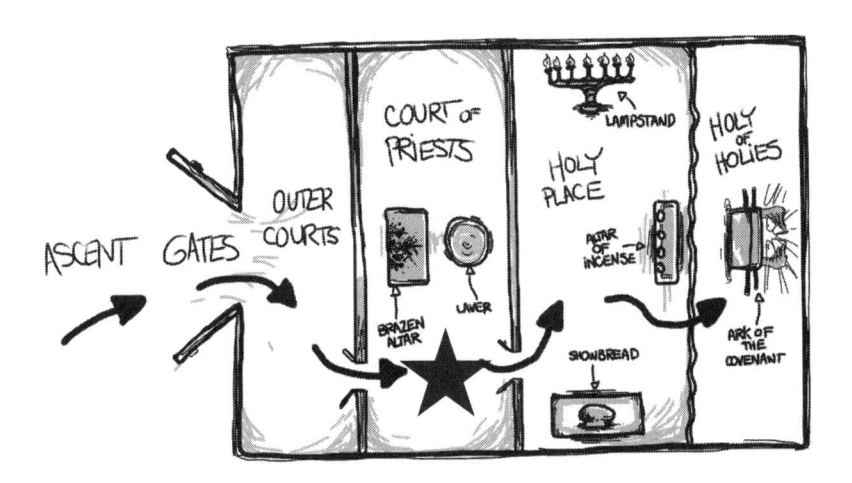

Stop.

Seriously, don't take another step. You're not allowed to go any further into the Temple. Only priests and Levites can enter the inner courtyards. Only priests can perform the sacred sacrifices and serve in the Holy Place. Only the High Priest can breach the Holy of Holies.

You? You're nobody special. No, you'll have to wait outside while the spiritual elite go deeper with God. Don't take it personally. It is what it is.

At least, that's what life was like before Jesus.

Don't be too jealous of the priests and Levites, though; they didn't have it much better than we do. To be a priest, you had to be born into the bloodline of the first priest, Moses' brother Aaron. Korah and sons were Levites who served during the Old Testament era. The Temple duties were divided among these

Temple workers and a kind of schedule was drawn up so everyone knew their place in the rotation.

Imagine having to wait your turn to serve in the Temple. One of Korah's sons once said, "How lovely is your dwelling place, O Lord Almighty. My soul yearns, even faints, for the courts of the Lord" (Psalm 84:1). Between shifts, being closer to God in the Temple was all he could think about. It drove him crazy. He goes on to confess with a sigh, "Better is one day in your courts than a thousand elsewhere" (Psalm 84:10).

That number wasn't drawn out of thin air. Korah's son apparently had to wait a thousand days between his allotted turns to serve in the Temple courts. A thousand days. That's nearly three years! And in his words, those solitary days in God's courts were more than just worth waiting for. They were the highlight of his entire life. Imagine Korah's son listening to us muttering about "having to" spend time with God because that's what good Christians do. I think he might just lay us out with an uppercut.

And again, that was before Jesus.

What Jesus did

When Jesus Christ died on the cross for our sins, he changed everything.

> Christ did not enter a sanctuary made with human hands that was only a copy of the true one; he entered heaven itself, now to appear for us in God's presence. Nor did he enter heaven to offer himself again and again, the way the high priest enters the Most Holy Place every year with blood that is not his own. Otherwise Christ would have had to suffer many times since the creation of the world. But he has appeared once for all at the culmination of the ages to do away with sin by the sacrifice of himself. Just as people are destined to die once, and after that to face judgment, so Christ was sacrificed once to take away the sins of many;

and he will appear a second time, not to bear sin,
but to bring salvation to those who are waiting for
him. (Hebrews 9:24-28).

Beautiful. This means the sacrificial altar of the Temple's court of priests has been replaced by something infinitely more powerful —the cross of Christ. It's no longer a place of sacrifice, but of grace. A place where sins are wiped away, where hearts are cleansed, where second chances are handed out like candy tossed to ecstatic children at a birthday party. The sacrifice of Jesus didn't just pay our way to heaven. It paved the way for us to approach God directly and intimately. No rotation, no waiting, no "better is one day in your courts." One day is every day, any time of day, for all eternity.

What we can do with what Jesus did

This is where the gospel gets real for us.

The "cross court" is one of my favourite spaces in the whole world. Every morning I come to the cross and confess the sins I know I've committed. I pour out my heart until I sense I've been totally real and transparent, holding nothing back.

But because I'm so forgetful, I also offer a prayer something like David prayed in Psalm 139:23,24: "Search me, God, and know my heart; test me and know my anxious thoughts. See if there is any offensive way in me, and lead me in the way everlasting." I invite God to shine the light of his truth on my heart to remind me of things I thought, said, and did that are sinful and fall short of his glorious ideal for my life.

The Apostle John says,

> "If we walk in the light, as he is in the light, we have
> fellowship with one another, and the blood of Jesus,
> his Son, purifies us from all sin. If we claim to be
> without sin, we deceive ourselves and the truth is
> not in us. If we confess our sins, he is faithful and

just and will forgive us our sins and purify us from
all unrighteousness" (I John 1:7-9).

When he shows me something to confess (and he always does) I just agree with him about it. That's what confession is: He says, "That's sin." I say, "You're absolutely right. I've sinned." The more I agree with God, the more like Jesus I become.

I want you to notice something though: David asked God to show him his "offensive *ways.*" John talked about "*walking* in the light." This is because that sin we confessed isn't just something we *did*; it's something we *do.* Most of our confession involves stuff that comes up again and again as a way of life.

At it's core, that sinful way of life is really about swapping something—anything, really—for God. Since mankind fell into sin in the garden of Eden, we've been trading God for ambition, lust, greed, you name it. Paul says we "became fools and exchanged the glory of the immortal God for images... (we) exchanged the truth of God for a lie, and worshipped and served created things rather than the Creator" (Romans 1:22,23,25). Bottom line, we've made swapping out Jesus for other stuff a way of life.

So when you confess a sin, ask God to show you who or what you've been trusting in instead of Jesus. It could be your own strength, or security, or maybe your friends and family. Whatever it is, even if it's a good thing, that substitute is an idol. So tell God you reject it as first in your life. Turn to him, turn to Jesus, and invite him to take the idol's place in your heart. You are forgiven.

Here's the great part: To forgive means to release, to cancel a debt. Another sense of the word means "to lift up and carry away." When we confess our sin, Jesus releases us from our guilt and the power sin idols have over us. He lifts our guilt and shame from our souls and carries it away. Forgiveness is a transaction, a real, live, powerful, tangible transaction with God. He takes our guilt and replaces it with grace. He lifts our shame and replaces it with peace.

When I confess my sin, I picture this stuff actually happening... because it actually is. I thank God for his grace, for his forgiveness, and imagine myself released from my guilt and shame. I thank God that I am pure and clean because his blood paid for my sin. Sometimes I picture being washed by a beautiful waterfall of grace. Or envision Christ lifting the burden from my shoulders. I always praise him again for his perfect cleansing work.

And I *feel* forgiven. How tragic would it be for Jesus to die on the cross for my sin and leave me miserable wretch, sulking around in my shame? No way! I park my soul at the cross as long as it takes for me to receive cleansing and forgiveness for every sin I've committed. If you still feel guilty for something, it's because the transaction isn't complete. Either you aren't done confessing it, or you haven't given him your guilt and shame. Don't move on until you've experienced the life-changing forgiveness of Jesus Christ. Until your heart is free and you know it.

And until you've forgiven everyone you need to forgive. The Holy Spirit will show you people you're mad at, things that happened that hurt you, words that stung, people you thought you were okay with but must not be because you can't stop replaying the conflict in your mind.

"Oh, I've forgiven them," people tell me.

"Really? You still seem resentful. Like it still hurts you and you're still rehashing what happened."

"Well sure, but forgiveness is a decision, and so I've said it out loud. I've forgiven them. I just can't seem to let the emotions go." Until those emotions have been lifted and you're totally free, you're not done. Remember, forgiveness is a transaction. And forgiving others works exactly the same way as forgiving yourself.

When you forgive someone, you're giving Jesus permission to release that person who offended you. You're giving Jesus authority to release them from justice in your mind and heart. You're giving him permission to pick up and carry away the anger you're feeling towards them. The resentment. The bitterness. You'll know you've forgiven—know the transaction is complete—when those negative emotions have been replaced by love and peace.

Don't look at me like that, it's what Jesus does. Like I said, the cross court is awesome! And the gospel actually works.
This is also the place to reaffirm that your old self—your flesh, or sinful nature—has been crucified with Christ and no longer lives

(Galatians 2:20). That means it no longer defines you. The new, real you in Christ lives by faith, by the power of the Holy Spirit.

You are responsible to God for all the sin you just confessed, but at the same time, that sin no longer defines you. It's a part of your old self, which is no longer you.

Your new self is awesome. It "is being renewed in knowledge in the image of its creator" (Colossians 3:9). More to the point, "your new self (is) created to be like God in true righteousness and holiness" (Ephesians 4:22-24). As you live from your new self, you're like Jesus. As you live from your old self, you sin. When you come to the cross in the court of priests, remind yourself of these truths and resolve to live them out.

Back to Korah

But wait—didn't I say that in Korah's day, only priests could enter this inner court? Yeah, I did. So did Jesus change all that? Nope. The rule still stands.

Look, anyone can pray ascent prayers. Everyone can enter the outer courts with a praise and a thank-you. But not just anyone can march their way into the Holy Place or darken the door of the Holy of Holies. Not on your life!

But then...how—?

John puts it this way: "To those that received (Christ), to those that believed in his name, he gave the right to become children of God" (John 1:12). We are children of God, born into the bloodline of Jesus Christ, the great High Priest. Which makes every one of us, God's children...priests in the King of King's family lineage. This is why Peter declares we "are a chosen people, a royal priesthood, a holy nation, God's special possession, that you may declare the praises of him who called you out of darkness into his wonderful light" (I Peter 2:9).

As a child of God, a fully-empowered priest of the kingdom, you have full access to the inner courts, the Holy Place, and even the Holy of Holies. The moment Jesus died, remember what happened? The heavy curtain sealing off the Holy of Holies ripped in two, from top to bottom. Only priests can go in there. Good thing you're a priest.

Which means that as fantastic as the cross is, and as important as it is to come to the cross and revel in the finished work of Jesus, we need to go deeper. The cross isn't an end in itself. It opens the way into the Holy Place, and beyond that…well, I'm getting ahead of myself.

Chapter 5
The Holy Place

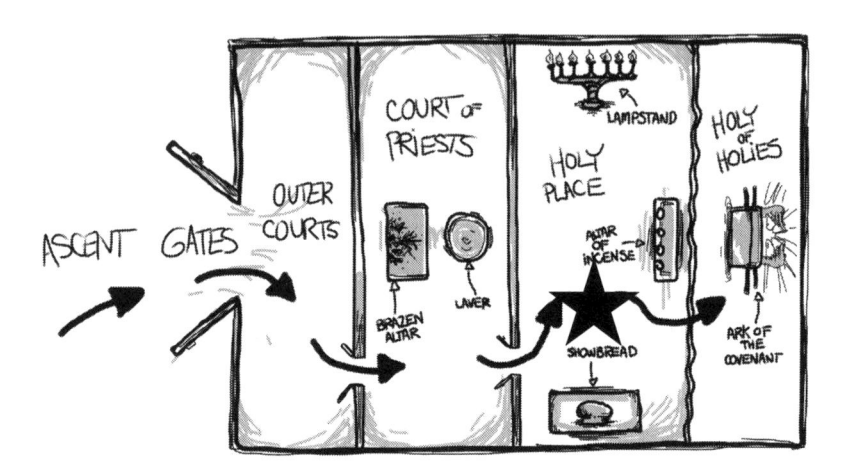

[Diagram of the tabernacle layout showing: Ascent, Gates, Outer Courts, Court of Priests (with Brazen Altar and Laver), Holy Place (with Lampstand, Altar of Incense, and Showbread), and Holy of Holies (with Ark of the Covenant).]

So far, if you've gone with the flow, you've unloaded the concerns of your heart and humanity to God. You've focused your mind on him through thankfulness and praise. You've confessed your sin and have been purified by the unfathomable grace of God poured out through the cross of Christ. And you're ready to go deeper.

So good, right?

Stepping into the Holy Place, you notice three beautiful pieces of furniture: a lampstand to your left, a table set to your right, and an altar sitting directly ahead. Each piece is a powerful symbol. Each symbol is an invitation into a life-changing experience with God through Jesus Christ.

Let's unpack this.

The lampstand

Turning to your left, you face a lampstand crafted from pure gold. Seven branches fan out from the base, curving upwards into golden almond blossoms open to the heavens. In each of the seven blossoms, candle flames are flickering. Twice a day, the priests trim the wicks and replenish the pure olive oil feeding the lamp stand. The flames never stop burning (Exodus 27:20,21).

The lampstand was an exquisite physical promise symbolizing God's everlasting presence with us. The priest's daily 'lamp duties' symbolize our part in cultivating our awareness of God's presence in our lives. Deuteronomy 31:8 says, "The Lord himself goes before you and will be with you; he will never leave you nor forsake you. Do not be afraid; do not be discouraged." And now because of Jesus, we can abide (live) in Christ and he in us (John 15:5). Our very lives are hidden in Christ, in God himself (Colossians 3:3).

In the Holy Place, we remind ourselves of this unshakeable reality and claim God's promised presence in a fresh way. We meditate on scriptures that proclaim this promise. We take time to thank God for being with us, that we are never alone.

The showbread

To your right, directly across from the lampstand, sits an ornate table overlaid with pure gold. The table displays a fresh loaf of bread replaced weekly by the priests on duty (Exodus 25:23-30). The bread is kept under a bowl to keep it fresh. The bread is a practical, physical promise symbolizing God's faithfulness in providing our needs.

Jesus himself is the bread of life (John 6:35). He promises to meet our needs, drawing endless blessings from his riches in glory so he can share them with us (Philippians 4:19). Here we seek his kingdom above all else, trusting he will meet all our practical needs as we follow him (Matthew 6:33).

In the Holy Place, we affirm God's continuous care for us and revel in his promise of love.

Throughout scripture bread also symbolizes the life and spiritual energy we get when we "eat" (study, digest, and obey) the Word of God. Jesus even said, "Man shall not live by bread alone, but by every word that comes from the mouth of God" (Matthew 4:4).

Because this is true, we dedicate special time to listen to the Holy Spirit for God's word. Think of it like the freshly baked bread of life he wants to share with you. A feast for your soul.

An important note: God will speak to you throughout this Temple flow time. As you move through the flow, he will bring scriptures to mind, offer direction, share important insights about your life, and reveal more of who he is. That said, the table of showbread reminds us to pause and reflect on the unique and flawless words of God revealed in the Bible, his written word. When God speaks, he creates amazing things. Like the cosmos, for example (Genesis 1:1). So whatever you do, let him speak! James tells us in plain English how to study God's word:

> "**Do** not merely **listen** to the word, and so deceive yourselves. **Do** what it says. Anyone who **listens** to the word but does not **do** what it says is like a man who **looks** at his face in a mirror and, after **looking** at himself, goes away and immediately forgets what he **looks** like. But the man who **looks** intently into the perfect law that gives freedom, and continues to do this, not forgetting what he has **heard**, but **doing** it - he will be blessed in what he **does**" (James 1:22-25).

James uses variations of three action words over and over again in this passage: Look, listen, and do. So take his advice! When you study, look—and look *intently*. Look for what the author says and what the passage truly means. And don't stop until you see yourself, your life, your situation, in the mirror. When you've seen something that applies to your life, listen. Listen to the Holy

Spirit for how and when he wants you to put it into practice. And then ask him for power, and then *do it.*

There's more to Bible study than that, obviously—but everything else is built on this simple progression: Look, listen, and do.

The altar of incense

Directly in front of you, flanked by the golden lampstand to your left and the table of showbread to the right, is an altar where priests like you burn incense to God. The room is already filled with the aroma as it wafts into every corner of the Holy Place.

The altar of incense is a physical symbol of prayer. Remember how Jesus himself passed through a heavenly tabernacle as he won our salvation? When John the Apostle got a day trip to heaven through an amazing vision, he saw the heavenly version of the incense and described it this way: "Then I saw a Lamb, looking like it had been slain, standing in the centre of the throne, encircled by the four living creatures… each one had a harp and they were holding golden bowls full of incense, which are the prayers of the saints" (Revelation 5:6,8).

"Wait a minute," I can hear you saying. "I've already prayed, during ascents. Remember? Didn't that count?"

I guess you could call that other stuff praying. But it was more like raw venting. That was God meeting you where you were at. Now you've been drawn deeper, to the place where God wants you to be.

Let's review: You've thanked and praised him. You've been forgiven and have forgiven others. You've been cleansed by his grace. And now you're standing to pray…with the promise of God's presence on one hand and his promise to provide on the other. Wow! You may have *prayed* before, but not like this.

And there's more. Our prayers are offered at an altar. An altar is place of surrender. Which is why Jesus taught us to pray, "Our father in heaven, holy be your name. Your kingdom come, your will be done, on earth as it is in heaven" (Matthew 6:9,10). True prayer is about us submitting to the rule of God in our lives. It's about making Jesus' dreams come true and coming to a place where we're longing for the same things he is.

So yes, lay your requests before God. But in the Holy Place, you're praying from the posture God wants from you. This is where mountains move, where miracles are unleashed, where the Word of God becomes the will of God in your life. Praying from this posture becomes more of a conversation with God than the grocery list you offered him on the way up the hill. So don't rush things.

Speaking of the grocery list, now would be a great time to come back to the things you vented during your ascent. You'll see them differently now. Take time to listen to God address what you shared earlier. Ask him, "What would you like me to know about this?" Then listen for his word, and deliberately bring these things to God in prayer.

For example, you might have vented about your idiot coworker during ascent: "Bob makes me so mad. He totally threw me under the bus again during staff meeting!" But then you took a few minutes to thank and praise God for his goodness to you.

Next, you came to the cross and realized your response to Bob was over-the-top. You also forgave Bob for his outburst and let the grace of God wash over you.

Now, in the Holy Place, you come back to the conflict and invite God's perspective on what happened. You pray for the relationship to be restored. You pray for a better attitude and patience to deal with him next time. You sense God's deep love for him and pray he would one day respond to Christ and become a believer.

Personally, I find keeping all this straight in my head tiring, so I keep a prayer journal. Writing stuff down gives me a way to refer back to what I vented during ascent. It also gives me a way of reviewing the past week, month, and even year. If journaling isn't your thing and you don't feel the need to hold on to any paper, jotting brief notes on a sticky-note could work. After you're done praying, toss it and move on.

The Holy Place is a powerful place to pray because we're far more likely to pray according to God's will. So make bold requests. As you pray, remember God has promised to be with you and provide for you. Pray with that in the front of your mind, infusing your faith with supernatural expectation. The writer of the book of Hebrews says,

> "We do not have a high priest who is unable to sympathize with our weaknesses, but we have one who has been tempted in every way, just as we are—yet was without sin. Let us then approach the throne of grace with confidence, so that we may receive mercy and grace in our time of need" (Hebrews 4:14-16).

When do you stop praying? The answer, for me at least, is simple: I pray until I can't think of anything else to pray about. Until my heart has been totally released from every trace of confusion, anxiety, anger, frustration, guilt, shame, distraction, and concern. If you remember another sin to confess, confess it and receive God's grace.

If another issue comes up, talk to God about it and give it to him in prayer. If he brings up another issue, explore it. If he shares another scripture, study it. Keep going until there's nothing left. Until your mind and heart are at rest.

Yes, it's possible. And it's beautiful. Best of all, it prepares us for the climax of the entire Temple flow: the Holy of Holies.

Chapter 6
The Holy of Holies

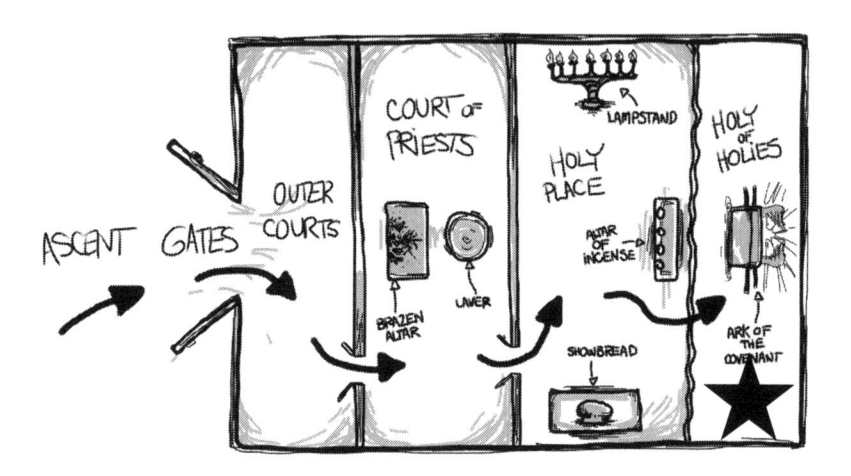

I began this book by saying that we can access God anywhere at any time. And that's true. Unfortunately, we're usually so full of ourselves when we access him that we often can't see, hear, and experience him in all his glory. Struggles, worries, frustrations, questions, conflicts, flighty emotions, temptations, negative thoughts, screwball ideas...on any given day, we're a mess. Am I right? And then we sit down and try to focus on God. Try to ignore all our issues. Try to be spiritual.

And fail. And fail. And fail.

And give up on meaningful time with God.

Until now.

Have you ever been to a movie where some idiot in the theatre won't shut up? He won't stop talking. He won't stop moving. He keeps getting up to stretch. He drives you nuts, right? You can't enjoy the movie because his distraction is taking centre-stage. Eventually you lose your cool and bark out orders: "Down in front!"

Intimacy with God is like that. I hope you can see the truth by now: Your only hope for enjoying God is to process all the distracting junk on the front of your mind so he can take its place. Going with the flow is designed to facilitate that "down in front" miracle. Once your tangled brain is settled, you're free to step into the Holy of Holies, where there's no thing—and no one—but God.

There are typically no prayer requests in the Holy of Holies. Just Jesus. There are no conflicts, just God's eternal glory. There are no questions, only speechless awe. There are no worries, only worship. There is no doing, only being. Bottom line, going with the flow frees us to forget ourselves in the presence of God. It releases us to do what the Westminster Confession claims is the chief end of man: to "enjoy God and glorify him forever."

How often do you think most Christians step into the Holy of Holies to simply enjoy God for who he is? Rarely? Never? There's a good reason for that. We park ourselves everywhere else and forget to move on. Or don't care to.

Some people settle for ascent prayers and never go much deeper. They vent to God like nobody's business, letting him have it when he disappoints them and telling him exactly what's on their minds. When they're in trouble, they huck prayers into the heavenlies like a Sunday morning preacher. But they never seem to get past their grocery list of self-centred requests.

Some people know God is listening and thank him for answered prayer. They praise the Father for being so attentive to their needs and thank him for his faithfulness in their lives. They even enjoy praise and worship music in church. Unfortunately, they never seem to get around to facing their own sinfulness and need for growth.

Some people—many church people, actually—love to park their lives around the cross. They're genuinely thankful for what Jesus has done and spend their lives revelling in that. They confess sin, forgive others, revel in their unworthiness, and celebrate the day they came to Christ. Which is fantastic, except they never do get around to using what Jesus has done to do what Jesus commands them to do next.

Still others apply the power of the cross to their relationship with God and learn to pray in faith, flanked by the promise of his presence and his lavish provision. They study his word and listen to the Holy Spirit as he guides them through the ups and downs of life. But they rarely or never experience God for who he is.

Every step we've unpacked in the Temple flow so far is biblical and necessary. We're commanded to pour out our hearts before God, to praise and thank him, to confess our sin and forgive others, and lay our requests before him with faith-filled expectation. But we're also invited to go "higher up and further in," to take the final step of meeting with God face to face in the Holy of Holies:

> Therefore, brothers and sisters, since we have confidence to enter the Most Holy Place by the blood of Jesus, by a new and living way opened for us through the curtain, that is, his body, and since we have a great priest over the house of God, let us draw near to God with a sincere heart and with the full assurance that faith brings, having our hearts sprinkled to cleanse us from a guilty conscience and having our bodies washed with pure water. Let us hold unswervingly to the hope we profess, for he who promised is faithful. (Hebrews 10:20-23).

I can tell you from experience: It's crazy how easy it is to get what I need from God and unplug from my quiet time without marinating in the Holy of Holies first. I'm like the kid who comes home from school and leaves a trail on the floor made of stinky shoes, books, lunch garbage, muddy footprints, and a form my mom needs to sign by tomorrow. I stride right past her to snag a chocolate-chip cookie from the cookie jar, give her a peck on the cheek, bounce out of the kitchen and leave her standing there calling out, "Uh, I missed you too!"

Jesus died a gruesome death to give us life. One of the most staggering gifts that comes with that life is a mind-blowing treasure for our pleasure—the Holy of Holies. The Father wants us to get past our wants and needs, even past the Bible, to feast on him alone.

Knowing my self-centred tendencies, I don't consider my quiet time complete until I've spent at least a few minutes completely still before God with nothing on my mind but him. I've found that unless I bask in God's glory sometime in my day, I can't seem to live from my new self in Christ because my old self rears its ugly head more often.

Here are some important things I've learned along the way about spending time in the Holy of Holies.

Posture

I love to bow down before God. Like, flat on the floor. Prostrating myself before him reminds me of his hugeness and my smallness. I think anyone in the Holy of Holies who doesn't feel the urge to face plant has serious pride issues.

Throughout the Bible, the word "worship" actually means "to bow down before, to prostrate oneself before." And throughout the Bible, worshippers bowed—not just in their hearts, like we North Americans think is enough, but with their bodies. There's something humbling about this. There should be.

Try it sometime. Then keep doing it.

God is worthy.

Imagination

It really helps me to imagine myself in the Temple, stepping across the threshold from the Holy Place into the Holy of Holies. I often envision God waiting for me. I invite him to reveal himself to me with greater clarity. He often fills my imagination with an image of his glory—dancing flames, blinding light, liquid love, or electricity. I often get a visual image of God's power reaching out to me, engulfing me, filling me, or healing me. When that happens, I worship him even more. Interestingly enough, I've never 'seen' the same thing twice.

If you need help envisioning being in God's presence like this, meditate on some key scripture passages. Try Isaiah chapter 6 or Revelation chapters 1 and 4 to get you started. The throne room in heaven is the spiritual equivalent of the Holy of Holies on earth, but infinitely more awesome.

Feeling it... or not

Personally speaking, I'm not usually overwhelmed with emotion in the Holy of Holies. The overriding sensation for me is usually a simple peace and a sense that I've been centred in Christ.

In the same way, it's rare for me to feel God physically. But that's okay. Feeling God is not the point. Worshipping him is.

What to do there

Sometimes I speak words of prayer and worship. Other times, I just behold him and revel in his awesomeness. I love to focus on aspects of his character—his holiness, his beauty, his love, his perfection.

At times, music is incredibly helpful for worship. But make sure the song you're using is a 'Holy of Holies' song. Most church music is focused on the first four elements of the flow—ascent, thanksgiving, the cross, and requests. True worship music talks to God personally vs. just talking about him. It's focused solely on who God is, not what he can do for us.

Now what?

Biblically, when people truly met with God like this, face-to-face, the stress they came with evaporated. This wasn't usually because their issue was resolved, but because God is so great that their mountain become a molehill in his presence. When we're lost in God's awesomeness, we tend to forget what was so all-consuming a few minutes earlier.

Another common result of being with God in the Holy of Holies is a renewed sense of clarity and call. We approach him with what's on our mind, but we leave captured by what's on his. Isaiah was commissioned from this most Holy Place. John received a vision, what we now call the book of Revelation—and a call to share it with the rest of the world. The other day while I was basking in his holiness, God said, "Get up, son, and go bless someone." So I did, and it was incredible. Remember, we're all priests now. Our mission is to help others get right with God through Jesus Christ. That's what priests do.

The deal is, you were made to worship. If you've gone with the flow, you'll be able to worship without your own issues distracting your mind and obscuring your view of his glory.

There's nothing on earth like it.

Chapter 7
Rhythm

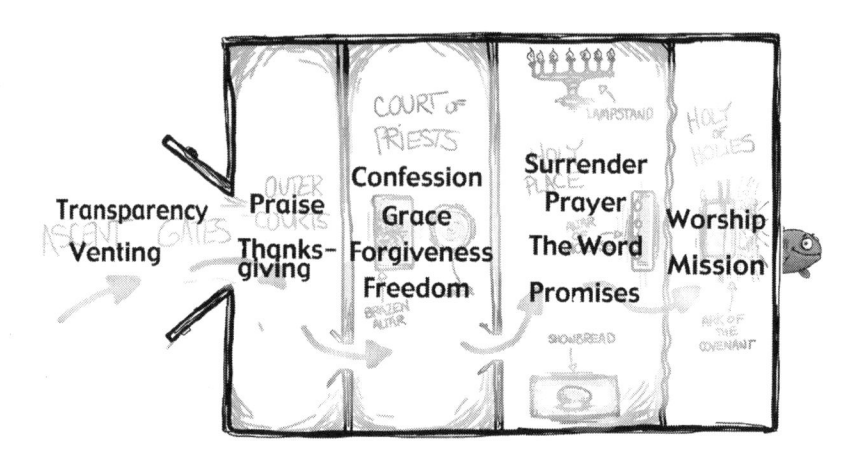

Transparency — **Praise** — **Confession** — **Surrender** — **Worship**
Venting — **Thanks-giving** — **Grace** — **Prayer** — **Mission**
— — **Forgiveness** — **The Word** —
— — **Freedom** — **Promises** —

(Diagram labels: OUTER COURTS, ASCENT, GATES, COURT OF PRIESTS, BRAZEN ALTAR, HOLY PLACE, LAMPSTAND, SHOWBREAD, HOLY OF HOLIES, ARK OF THE COVENANT)

    As you can now see, going with the flow provides the focus you'll need to have a balanced relationship with God. All the things we've talked about are built right in.
    In particular, going with the flow guides us through a God-inspired process that helps us get over ourselves, to exchange our brokenness and idolatry for Christ's abundant life and glory. The beauty of the flow is that it weaves all these elements into a memorable and repeatable pathway. As we walk the path, we're led into our heart's deepest desire—God himself.
    But the Temple flow isn't dummy-proof, so let me warn you about a few common traps to avoid.
    Because they really are traps, and you'll be tempted to fall into them.

1. The 'whole enchilada' trap

A funny thing happened on the way to the New Testament: The Hebrews missed the whole point of the Temple flow.

Actually, somewhere along the way the flow *became* the point. The end in itself, instead of a means to an end. A flow is supposed to lead you somewhere, right? Going with the flow is supposed to saturate our entire lives with Christ and his gospel.

When my kids first started learning to ride a bike, we slapped training wheels on the sides. The training wheels freed them to learn the strange dance of pedalling, turning, braking, and balance with less fear of falling.

I'll never forget the day we took off the training wheels off our son Noah's first bike. I set him up with his bum on the seat, feet on the pedals. My job was to hold onto the back of the bike and run behind him until he was ready for me to let go.

"Okay, buddy," I explained. "What I want you to do is start pedalling, but don't wo—"

Wheeee!

Before I could stop him, he took off. I mean, he pedalled the bike right out of my hands and just…rode the thing. My jaw dropped as I watched him bob, weave, and pump his way down the sidewalk without me, without the training wheels.

He was free!

He wiped out eventually, and not for the last time, either. But that didn't matter anymore. He was too thrilled to be discouraged. He'd experienced the power, rhythm and momentum of riding a bike, felt the wind in his hair, and tasted big-boy freedom.

Eventually he learned he didn't even need to be pedalling the whole time to stay upright. He could glide, skid, pop wheelies, and kathunk over curbs.

That can be you, too.

Your quiet time with God is your bike, and the Temple flow is your training wheels. Your relationship with God must grow beyond the routines we use to keep us on track. He'll use it to soften your heart to him so he can get to you anywhere at any time. Once you taste the freedom, you'll never depend on devotional books again.

2. The 'only way' trap

After experiencing the power of going with the flow, we might be tempted to think it's the only way to spend time with God. We might even make it a rule or even a law and judge ourselves and others based on that law. I think you can see this would be missing the point. There is nothing in scripture that commands us to use the Temple flow exactly the way I've outlined it. There is no black and white verse that judges our relationship with God based on how well or how often we do it.

What we do have in scripture is a personal invitation from God to approach him in a way he custom designed to help us thrive. We have an opportunity to learn how to ride our quiet time bike with joy, to learn the spiritual rhythms we'll need to walk with Christ for the rest of our lives.

At first, your quiet time will benefit from pedalling to a clear routine. A routine is designed to help you find your rhythm. But once you find your rhythm, you have to be careful, because routines quickly become life-sucking ruts.

Once you've tasted how amazing the rhythms of God's kingdom really are, you won't need your training wheels on your quiet time. You'll know all this stuff and do it instinctively. And once you've learned to ride the Temple flow bike, you won't forget how.

You may get rusty, but within a few minutes after dusting it off, you're sailing along again with little effort and a lot of joy.

3. The 'quiet time script' trap

Going with the flow uses a path, not a script. It gives us direction, not directions. In fact, if you're being real with God, every single quiet time will play out differently.

Some days, your opening line is going to be, "I'm so sorry I lost my temper." Other days, the first thing on your mind might be something you're thankful for, or something about God you want to praise him for. In other words, the first three elements—ascent, thanksgiving, and forgiveness—are going to happen as they happen. Don't get locked into a script. Go with the flow.

In the same way, if you're actually connecting with God instead of going through the motions, he's going to be speaking, guiding, and leading you in unique ways. Throughout the Bible, no two encounters with the living God were the same. Why would it be any different with us?

And remember who's in charge. If Jesus wants to spend an hour unpacking a Bible passage, go with it. If he wants you to be still and know that he is God, be still. If you feel drawn to worship before you 'get to' the Holy of Holies, fall to your knees and do it. If you're in the Holy of Holies and he reminds you of a sin you've committed, confess it! A guy I know became so peaceful in the Holy of Holies he fell asleep. Isn't that awesome? The Temple flow isn't about the order as it is about the intimacy. And the divinely inspired variety keeps it fresh day after day.

Just this morning, as I was preparing to go with the flow, I felt prompted to play a familiar worship song on my laptop instead. In my mind's eye I was drawn into the throne room almost immediately, where I experienced a beautiful vision of our glorious God. I also received a powerful impartation I can hardly wait to share with the world. Praise him!

In Psalm 23, David reflects on the rich variety he experienced along his spiritual journey. First, he framed it all by declaring, "The Lord is my shepherd. I won't lack anything." He knew if God was leading him, he'd always get what he needed to be faithful, no matter where the trail led. Sometimes he was led to lie down in green pastures. Other times, he was invited to drink from quiet streams. Other times he found himself following through dark, lonely valleys—or fighting enemies in dangerous battles. But through it all, his cup overflowed and he knew he would dwell in God's presence forever (see Psalm 23).

David understood that relationship with God is about rhythms, not routines. And certainly not scripts.

4. The 'checklist' trap

After experiencing the power in each of the elements in the Temple flow, you might be tempted to think of your quiet time as a series of things you need to do in succession. And while it's good for us to experience all the elements along the pathway, your time with God is not a checklist.

> Ascent? Check.
> Thanksgiving? Check.
> Forgiveness? Check.
> Surrendered prayer? Oops, forgot that one. Sorry, God.

Going with the flow isn't about checking things off a list so we can feel good about ourselves. It's not about "Devotional correctness." It's about walking with Jesus in all of life.

It would also be really easy to view the entire quiet time itself as something to check off a daily to-do list. *There, I did my God time. Now I can do my own thing for the rest of my day.* But remember, going with the flow helps us live our entire lives saturated, empowered, and guided by God. It's not something to "get done." It's about being the little fish on the cover of this book. We swim into the kingdom river and let the current take us where it takes us.

I also love the bike analogy I mentioned earlier. Bike riders know pedalling *consistently* is important. They also know pedalling *constantly* misses the point. The point is movement—getting from A to B. And just like bike riding, the fun part is actually gliding and improvising. I love cresting a hill after pumping hard, sitting back and enjoying the breeze as momentum carries me forward. The key to enjoyable biking is knowing when to pedal, how hard to pedal, and when to relax and enjoy the ride. It's the same with your relationship with God.

When you do the same thing over and over again, it eventually gets old. So ditch the checklist.

5. The 'all or nothing' trap

When I unpacked this Temple flow in our small group, one of my friends said, "This is great, but I just don't have the time to do this every day." She's up early, home late, often brings work home, and has a husband to love on. How could she possibly find the time to meander through each element of the flow during such a busy schedule?

The temptation we all face is to throw the baby out with the bathwater, to give up on the idea entirely. I have two suggestions to avoid falling into this trap.

First, every moment you give love and attention to God counts. Some is better than nothing. Do what you can with what you have, and leave the rest to God. My challenge to my friend was simple: What if you set apart time to go with the flow once this next week?

She nodded. Once she could do.

Second, where have I ever said this has to take a long time? Some days I spend over an hour immersed in the flow. Other days I'm 'done' in fifteen minutes. I often do this several times a day for a few minutes each. Did you catch that? You could do this in two minutes if need be:

> "Lord, I'm really stressed about the conversation with _____. I mean, he's been a real tool lately (ASCENT). But I praise you for always being with me (PRAISE). And…you know what, I'm sorry for my own part in this conflict. I forgive him for his attitude. Slather the whole thing with your grace, Lord (FORGIVENESS & GRACE). Hmmm, that reminds me of I John 1:9. Thanks for your cleansing and grace (THE WORD). So… would you give me real insight into _____'s needs in this? I really want to be your light and love in this situation (SURRENDERED PRAYER). *I sense God's smile as I rest in him for thirty seconds, picturing his beautiful Spirit filling me with love and light* (WORSHIP). "I love you, Lord. Amen."

Like I said, two minutes. You'll get more out of the flow if you take your time, but again, something is better than nothing.

Chapter 8
Go With The Flow

Well, that's it.

In chapter one I said that if you want to experience God's love and power every day, you can. I said God has left the front door open and handed you the Temple flow to take you there. I promised that if you approach God using God's way during your quiet time, you can experience an intimacy with God you've only dreamed of until now. Walking with Jesus through the flow, you can:

- Get over yourself every day
- Be cleansed of all guilt and shame
- Focus your eyes on Jesus and what matters to him
- Live your life with God's perspective, in his presence, with his power
- Find release from yesterday's burdens
- Tune in to God's voice and guidance
- Free your mind of tomorrow's worries
- Enjoy God and develop a grateful, worshipful heart
- Enjoy a sacred space, even for just a few minutes a day, where you can simply adore, behold, and enjoy God for who he is instead of what he can do for you
- Be sent into each day as Jesus' hands and feet

But I've saved the best for last. You'll recall that, "When Christ came as high priest...he went through the greater and more perfect tabernacle that is not man-made, that is to say, not a part of this creation" (Hebrews 9:11). The earthly tabernacle and Temple were patterned after a spiritual, heavenly tabernacle.

Well, one day John, one of Jesus' Apostles, was transported to heaven and he recorded his vision in the book of Revelation. After his jaw-dropping grand tour of paradise, John said something a little weird. Something that seems to contradict what I've been saying in this book. He said, "I did not see a Temple in the city" (Revelation 21:22).

The real kicker is *why* there isn't a temple structure in heaven: "Because the Lord God Almighty and the Lamb are its temple" (Revelation 21:22).

Let that sink in: the heavenly flow of worship you've been using hasn't just been guiding you through a bunch of mental exercises. It's been ushering you deeper into God himself. The gates you enter open up experience with God. The "cross court" is within God's heart. The Holy Place is within God's grace. The Holy of Holies is within God's glory. Which means going with the flow helps you experience the reality that "in him we live and move and have our being" (Acts 17:28).

So by all means, have fun with this—and go with the flow. If you need a little help, you can use the "cheat sheet" on the last page.

About the Author
(That'd be me.)

Brad Huebert is a husband, father, church-planter, author, and geek who loves Jesus like crazy. He lives with his amazing wife, Shauna and three kids in Calgary, Alberta, Canada.

Brad's passion is to manifest Jesus Christ—his kingdom, his power, his love, his presence, his gospel… all for his glory. Because when Jesus is manifest…wow.

Okay, enough of the stuffy third-person schtick. I'd love to connect with you, so feel free to come find me online. See you soon!

- My website and blog: www.bradhuebert.com
- Facebook: www.facebook.com/christian.geeks
- Twitter: @GeekFaithTribe
- Pinterest: http://www.pinterest.com/bradhuebert/

ASCENT

Vent and pour out your heart to God. Don't hold anything back.

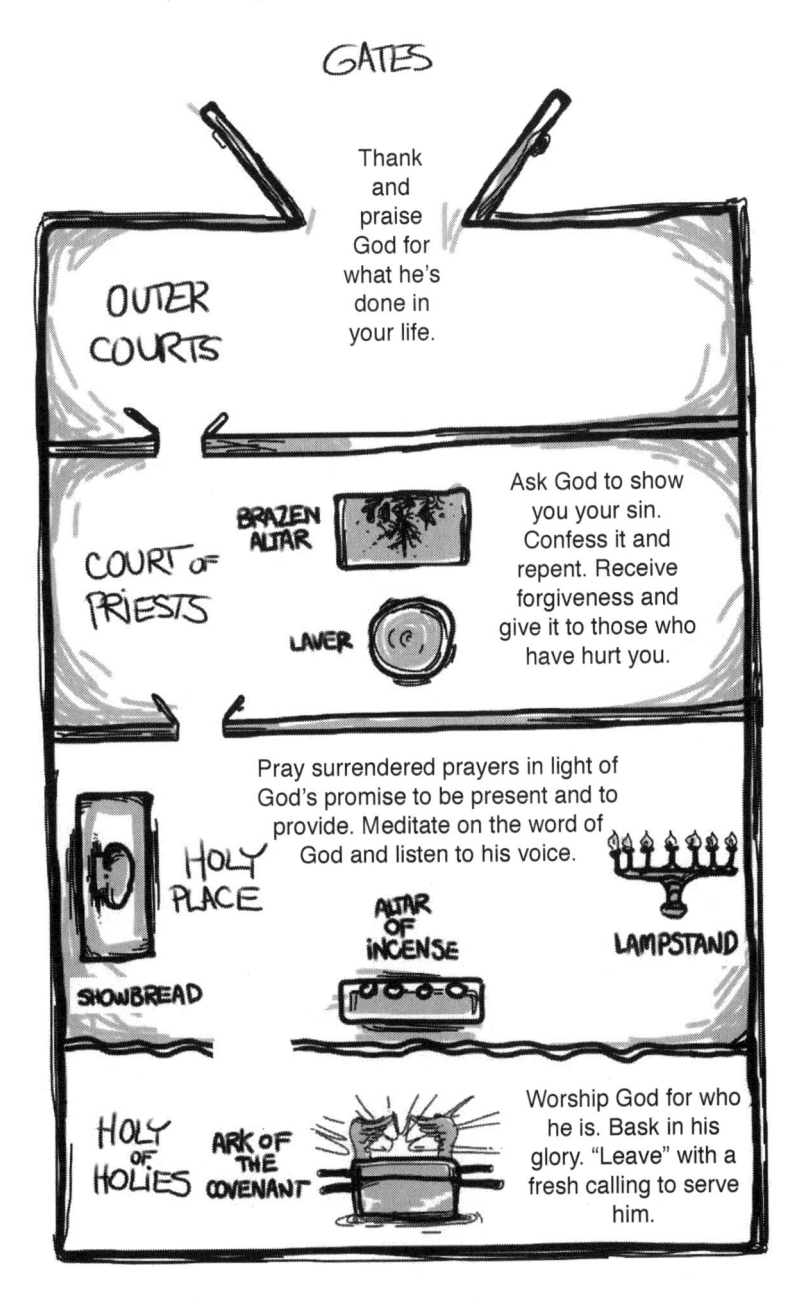

GATES

OUTER COURTS

Thank and praise God for what he's done in your life.

COURT OF PRIESTS

BRAZEN ALTAR

LAVER

Ask God to show you your sin. Confess it and repent. Receive forgiveness and give it to those who have hurt you.

HOLY PLACE

SHOWBREAD

ALTAR OF INCENSE

LAMPSTAND

Pray surrendered prayers in light of God's promise to be present and to provide. Meditate on the word of God and listen to his voice.

HOLY OF HOLIES

ARK OF THE COVENANT

Worship God for who he is. Bask in his glory. "Leave" with a fresh calling to serve him.

Made in the USA
Charleston, SC
02 August 2014